Reconstructing the Heart

Towards a Theology of Emotion

Reconstructing the Heart

Towards a Theology of Emotion

JASON M. GARWOOD

Cross & Crown Books
Warrenton, VA

Reconstructing the Heart: Towards a Theology of Emotion

Copyright 2019 © Jason M. Garwood

Publisher:
Cross & Crown Books
41 West Lee Highway
Suite 59 Box #199
Warrenton, VA 20186

Cover Design: Red Bag Media

Scripture quotations are from New Revised Standard Version Bible, copyright © 1989 National Council of the Churches of Christ in the United States of America. Used by permission. All rights reserved worldwide.

Printed in the United States of America.

ISBN-13: 978-1-7341228-0-0
ISBN-10: 1-7341228-0-3

DEDICATION

To the saints in Warrenton at
Cross & Crown Church:
May your pursuit of the Kingdom be
emotionally *charged.*

CONTENTS

ACKNOWLEDGMENTS

First, the glory belongs to God and his Christ. The Triune God gives us epistemological self-consciousness, and what's really impressive is that he tops it off with joy and happiness and *purpose*. It's a sweet deal, really.

I also want to thank my wife, Mary, for her unwavering support, love, and friendship; my children for being an absolute blessing; and the fine soldiers of Cross & Crown Church with whom it is a pleasure to go to war.

FOREWORD

"DON'T BE SO EMOTIONAL!" I'M SURE you've said this before, or at least maybe you've heard it. This type of reasoning is asserted with foremost confidence, affirmed with the utmost intention of squelching any perceived emotional *weakness*. Emotions, it is believed, are the fruits of fragility; they only come out when someone exhibits vulnerability or enfeeblement. To be strong, then, is to be rational and sensible, not *emotional.* Heaven forbid! "Don't cry like a little girl," one may say (as though girls are the only ones who give themselves over to such emotional concerns). The question before us, then, is: does this thinking square with God's law?

No. It doesn't. It doesn't fit within the parameters of the law-word of God because emotions are given to us from the hand of the Creator God who *has them too.* It's not that we have to decide between *having* emotions or *not having* emotions. Rather, we are privileged to reflect God by experiencing and delivering the *correct* ones. God doesn't struggle with emotional inconsistencies. He isn't given over to fits of rage after spilling the milk. He doesn't struggle with insecurity or lash out on others because of this or that reason. God emotes righteously and justly. And this means that we are called to do the very same thing.

The book you have in your hand has been carefully crafted to be a balance of practical wisdom and theological precision. There's a lot of technical words and phrases and concepts and the reader is invited to further study them. I have also tried to not just explain the concepts but demonstrate how they might apply. The reader will have to be the judge on how well I did.

One thing I will say at the outset, and I know of no author who would be hesitant to say such things: this book is not to be seen as the final word on the matter. God's Word is the only final word. These words are simply meant to be an exploration of the concepts and no doubt things may be left undone. I eagerly admit that much more needs to be said in this area, and perhaps someone else can take up the task.

Having said all that, I pray that you are blessed and encouraged as you explore what it means to reconstruct the heart.

Jason Garwood
Warrenton, VA
October 28, 2019

1

WHOLE BODY, WHOLE GOSPEL

Then God said, "Let us make humankind in our image, according to our likeness; and let them have dominion over the fish of the sea, and over the birds of the air, and over the cattle, and over all the wild animals of the earth, and over every creeping thing that creeps upon the earth." So God created humankind in his image, in the image of God he created them; male and female he created them. God blessed them, and God said to them, "Be fruitful and multiply, and fill the earth and subdue it; and have dominion over the fish of the sea and over the birds of the air and over every living thing that moves upon the earth."
Genesis 1:26-28

IT'S RARE TODAY TO FIND MEN AND women as passionate as David when he confidently fought the beast named Goliath, or as undignified as David was that time he stood before the ark of the covenant. Few and far between do we find people wholly undone as was Jeremiah when he preached to the wayward nation of Israel. And to think, I haven't even mentioned the time when Jesus threw hands with the moneychangers in the temple. Okay, so it wasn't hands that were thrown *per se*, but you know what I mean. (He had whips....*in his hands*. You're not even allowed to use those in *MMA* fights!)

The reason that passion and zeal seem to have waned in today's evangelical world is because our theology of the heart and emotion is thoroughly broken.

- We have post-Enlightenment *rationalism* repackaged and taking root in the Church. (e.g., mind as central and supreme component to the Christian life, 'catechism answers only' environment, etc.)

- We have a revival of *paganism* and its accompanying fertility cult infiltrating the Church and spreading death and destruction. (e.g., sex is god, homosexuality, abortion, etc.)

- We have the faulty presuppositions of *Greek philosophy* reappearing in Christian theology, scholarship and practice.

- We have *existentialism* permeating the minds

of the people of God. (e.g., Man and reason and his freedom/autonomy is the most important thing over against God and his glory, etc.)

In short: because we lack a biblical foundation on things like psychology, philosophy, and theology, the culture around us is rapidly deteriorating, and no one seems to know what to do.

The answer to any worldview that contradicts the Bible is...*the Bible*. The Word of God and the authority it brings to every philosophy or psychology is the antidote to all non-Christian thought. As Cornelius Van Til has taught us, all non-Christian thought is inherently dialectical—it cannot resolve or synthesize seemingly contradictory concepts like the individual and collective, universal and particular, or faith and reason. Only when we start with the ontological Trinity can we sort out the uncertainty. The way to combat paganism and naturalism and the cults is to preach the gospel of the Kingdom of the Triune God and all of its presuppositions, authority, logic, and truth. And, coincidentally, it's also the way we combat those inconsistencies in our minds and in our emotions.

Since this is a book on the psychology of man

and the role of emotions in our being, we're not necessarily going to delve deep into these other non-Christian worldviews. We *are* going to touch on them to some degree in order to gauge just how serious they have affected us, but this shouldn't be considered to be a full-blown treatise on such things. I'll leave that to other scholars with more time on their hands.

Having said all of that, the question before us is this: What is man? And not just *what*, but *who*: Who is man? Who is man in relation to the world? Who is man in relation to himself—his emotions, thinking, and acting? More to the point, *who and what is man in his relationship to God?*

The foundation of Christianity and its expression in the world through man is the *heart*—the center of man, the inner man, the spring that dispenses the issues of life (Prov. 4:23). The heart is what makes you, *you*. Here in Proverbs 4:23, the Hebrew word is *lev* and its main meaning has to do with the locus of a person's entire being, his desires, emotions, volition, and thinking. In the Western world, we tend to think of the heart as being the emotional branch of the soul, and the brain as the thinking section. However, in the Hebraic world, the "heart" is the source from which *everything* flows. It is the heart that encompasses everything about man. The heart is grand central station for what it means to *exist*. (As a side note, the Hebrew worldview would sometimes describe the emotions as stemming from the bowels, kidneys, or even the liver. The "mind" was the "heart," while the emotions came from your digestive innards.)

Now, when God created man in his image, he did so with a particularly unique context and set of circumstances. Man is a *creature* and is the result of God's sovereign *action*. There is no self-actualization or self-directed existence; there is no evolutionary process. Because man was brought into existence in time and space by God meaning has been imputed to him. It is not as though he can create meaning out of thin air; he can try, but he will fail. God is the great *imputator*, not man. This is because man is *created* in the image of God; meaning is granted, not invented. There is no hypothetical or conceptual past whereby man can appeal to some vague, nebulous pre-existence. Man was *not*, but now he *is*, and that's because of *I AM*. Like Moses, we should say, "I AM sent me."

Given the fact that man is subordinate to the authority of God (man is the covenantal recipient not the covenantal agent or initiator) man's being and purpose and psychology is determined and fixed and unalterable. He is unable to ascend to the level of predestination power (though he will try); therefore, he must acknowledge God's transcendence, lest he become suicidal.

The other privilege of being created in the image of God is the fact that man was created upright. He was made righteous and holy and good. Man was not an accident, nor was he self-created in a condition of neutrality. Man was and is in covenant with God, and this means he was created *mature*. Being mature and in covenant with God meant that man is held responsible for his actions. He cannot blame his environment or circumstance on anything other than himself. He is a person, he is accountable, and he is liable to the courts of heaven.

Given the fact that all men and women are made equally in the image of God, we can also say that existence is very *good*. What is normal and healthy are things like righteousness and peace, holiness and wisdom. God is good, our existence is entirely derived from his goodness, which means the normal pattern for this existence is purpose, dominion, and emotional and physical health. It is *not* (as Sartrean existentialism likes to posit) that existence precedes essence; rather, *imputation governs and precedes essence* (and thus existence) because our essence is tied to the being and nature of God. God is, and we, as a consequence, *are*. God predestines, we respond. We don't have the freedom and authority to create our own existence; this desire for usurpation is a result of the fall. We have the right and freedom to either bend the knee to God or stand up straight, stiffen our necks, and clench our fists. We are not ultimately free to unilaterally declare ourselves to be "like God," knowing and determining good and evil for ourselves (Gen. 3:5). We are confined to God's self-revelation and this confinement is a feature, not a bug.

Now, the last thing I want to focus on as it pertains to the image of God has everything to do with man's calling and task of dominion. There is no proper reconstruction of the heart by the Spirit until we come to grips with this reality: you and I are creatures of the Creator, ordered to exercise dominion, subduing the earth through restoring men and women and institutions to proper obedience to the King, thus making them fit for the Kingdom. It's a renovation of the entire *cosmos*.

Dominion is frustrated by sin and since humanist psychology won't deal in terms of sin and ethics, it is helpless to put man back on track towards proper dominion and purpose, and thus the person is stuck in frustration with no relief in sight.

All of this is because humanist versions of psychology do not recognize the authority of God; it rejects the Creator/creature distinction, and thus leaves man without hope of healing and restoration. Man's task of dominion—when restored in Christ— gives man a purpose outside of himself, and thus removes any precondition for selfishness and pride.

When we speak of reconstructing the heart and developing a theology of emotion it is important to hold these distinctions in place. The Western world, influenced by Greek philosophy, oftentimes likes to play the dualism game, segregating man's ontology by relegating one aspect of existence to one particular organ. Because of the influence of the Enlightenment—which in large part was the reintroduction of Greek philosophy's presuppositions—man is forced back into the false dialectics of humanism. Let me explain.

For Plato and Aristotle and much of the ancient Grecian world, there was a great chasm between man as an Idea, and man as matter. The two dualistic realms became known as "Form" versus "Matter." There is *physical* man and his physical body with all its lusts, impulses, passions, and desires; and there is *metaphysical* man in the realm of ideas, concepts, and abstractions. For Plato and those who followed him this became in irresolvable problem. There is no synthesis of the two ideas. The only way out is to embrace the conceptual and have severe distaste for the physical. Suppress the emotions and don't let the desires shape you. Stick to the metaphysical postulations, etc. "Mind over matter," and so on.

In the pagan construction of the world the nature of being in anthropology is rooted in naturalism: man is a product of his environment. He has miraculously evolved and transitioned from cellular goo to epistemological self-consciousness. But has he?

In Christian theology, our construction of the world rests on the fact that man is not a product of time and chance, rather, he is a product of the living God. Man is made in the image of God; his being is predetermined and not left to chaos and his environment.

Getting these two things right is essential for dealing with our emotions. Handling depression, addiction, trials and debacles—all of it must be approached from the latter category and not the first. You are not a product of your environment. However, because of Neoplatonist ideas about the world, Christians have largely neglected in counseling and biblical/practical theology the need for understanding our environment. Rather than discarding the material world (because, after all, you must set your mind on things above!), we should embrace the environment around us and filter it through a proper theology. Which means that we must consider family of origin issues. We must consider the impact of government education in shaping most of us. We must consider the way our parents did or didn't teach us how to handle conflict, etc.

We must deal with the trauma: the hurt, the betrayal, the rejection, the feelings of being unloved or unwanted, and the pain. Like it or not, those things shape us and mold us—they are influencers, but not determiners. They impact us but they don't define us. We are made in the image of God, planted here to grow and mature and reflect God's thinking, God's feeling, and God's purposes. Don't reject the world, see it as broken and in need of restoration. The same can be said of you.

In this worldview the material is downplayed and suffocated under the weight of mans' thinking. Thus, you have the Stoic's who tamed their desires for pleasure altogether, and the Epicureans who loved pleasure but believed it needed to be tempered to some degree. For the latter, the only way to achieve *ataraxia*, or, tranquility, is to gain knowledge but keep your desires and emotions in constant check. The bottom line: the Greek philosopher-kings couldn't reconcile any of it, so they made their choice. Material? *Bad.* Abstraction? *Good.*

What started as Form vs. Matter turned into Nature vs. Grace, which turned into Reason & Science vs. Faith, and here we are today. The fruit of all of this pagan thinking is the belief that your emotions can't be trusted, your desires are inherently evil, and the only way forward is to exalt the mind. The Reformed world has been particularly unhelpful in promulgating Christian Rationalism: the elevation of the mind over emotions. But is this biblical? The short answer: no. The long answer will be our exploration throughout this book.

One final thing needs to be said. The great antithesis of human history as sovereignly orchestrated by God has been and is always *ethical.* It is Sin vs. Grace, the Autonomy of Man vs. the Theonomy of God. The antithesis is *never* metaphysical. The issue is always going to be ethics: is the thing in line with God's law-word, or is it a product of man's autonomy? Is the thing sinful, or is it in alignment with the holiness of God? It is never ever going to be Material vs. Conceptual. That is not the world God has created. And the reason for this is because we are made in the image of God and Jesus Christ has come to restore that image. We were created with a *whole* body, and we have a *whole* gospel to bring everything to health.

So why should we view man as a whole creature? Because Jesus is both God and Man: the Transcendent is also Immanent. He is distinct, yet near and identifiable. Whole body, whole gospel. We don't have to choose our minds over our emotions. We don't have to choose to rapture ourselves out of the physical. In Christ, we have it all. We are *whole*.

Because Jesus has come and unleashed his gospel on the created order, we can be assured that God does not want your emotions to be subdued and stuffed so that your mind can be the only thing in operation. He wants your emotions to be cleaned up and let loose: this is why scripture can say to be angry, but do not sin (Ephesians 4:26). Anger is a powerful emotion, but it isn't to be seen as intrinsically evil. It's an emotion that God himself possesses, one which we must learn to wield properly.

Whole body, *whole* gospel. These are the foundations. Much of this is technical but the rest of this will be far more practical. If we can get this right, we can build a healthy theology of emotion. The next thing we need to deal with, however, is *guilt.*

2
GUILT GIVE-AWAY

Then the eyes of both were opened, and they knew that they were naked; and they sewed fig leaves together and made loincloths for themselves. They heard the sound of the Lord God walking in the garden at the time of the evening breeze, and the man and his wife hid themselves from the presence of the Lord God among the trees of the garden.
Genesis 3:7-8

For whoever keeps the whole law but fails in one point has become accountable for all of it.
James 2:10

THE GREAT PROBLEM THAT BESETS MAN, the supremely exasperating complication that leaves man beleaguered in all of his existence and toiling is the search for somewhere to place his guilt. From the very beginning man was plagued with feelings of guilt; but long before the *feelings* came was the *objective reality*: man has sinned against God.

When Adam and Eve chose to break covenant with God they did so because of the temptation of autonomy: to know and determine good and evil for themselves (Gen. 3:5). Once the heart's desires are set in motion, the mind comes along to reason its justification. What the heart longs for the mind declares righteous and good. What the emotions crave the will sees to it that it comes to pass. This cycle of self-determination brought havoc to the soul of man and destruction to the created order. As Genesis 3 so clearly articulates, the entirety of our being has been tainted and cracked, polluted by sin. Like the mind our *emotional* state is affected by sin, too.

A byproduct to this covenantal apostasy and self-destruction is guilt: the eyes of Adam and Eve were opened, they knew that they were naked, and they felt shame and guilt, which led them to hide from the Lord. *Guilt makes us run.* Guilt, then, is paired with God's law because when there is a transgression of God's covenant, guilt is the necessary outcome.

Perhaps a working definition of guilt is in order. *Guilt is the covenantal state of transgressing the law of God which brings about feelings of insecurity and conviction due to a forsaking of responsibility and obedience to God.* Notice how James 2:10 frames it: when we break one law, we're guilty of them all. One violation means *wholesale* violation. Romans 3:19 spells this out as well: "Now we know that whatever the law says, it speaks to those who are under the law, so that every mouth may be silenced, and the whole world may be held accountable to God."

Because sin is by definition the transgressing of the law of God (1 John 3:4) and *not* the transgression of the feelings or arbitrary standards set up by men, we can conclude that guilt, which comes from the transgressing, is also as objective, actual, and defined as the law itself. Accompanying the law of God are the *consequences* of the law of God, and guilt and shame are at the forefront. In short: guilt presupposes responsibility and responsibility presupposes objectivity.

What God intends is for sin to have real-time repercussions. Because of sin our mouths are closed (what can we possibly say?) and we are guilty. We may murmur about this from time-to-time, but the murmuring doesn't remove the guilt. We may also blame our environment, like Adam and Eve, but our environment does not make us sin nor does blame-shifting remove the guilt. In other words, "Thus saith the Lord" comes long before what you think or what you feel.

Due to the comprehensive nature of life in God's world God saw fit to ensure that our rebellion receives due punishment. And the one powerful way God has chosen to do this is by administering guilt to those who have intruded upon his holiness. Guilt means that God, through the instrument of his law-word, taps you on the shoulder and says, "Enough already." It is a leash to keep us from going headlong into further sin and debauchery.

The comprehensive nature of guilt means that the entirety of our being is at risk of emotional instability. Objective guilt results in subjective feelings of guilt. Real covenantal violation results in emotional volatility. *This is a gift from God.* The whole reason guilt exists is to move someone away from it. True guilt, as opposed to false guilt, is a self-correcting feature of God's grace. Guilt is a grace whose intentions are pure. Guilt is designed to help you get away from itself.

Now, fallen man is a guilt-ridden man, and there will always be the desire to find ways to deal with this conundrum. Man will search high and low looking for somewhere to stash and stuff the guilt. Some will choose to ignore guilt and pile on the self-condemnation. Others, like Freud, will divorce guilt from sin and instead notify the world that it's now a *biological* problem only. The third and only real option is to run to Christ, but now we're getting ahead of ourselves.

Sigmund Freud (1856-1939) believed in the supreme power of self-analysis and psychoanalysis. By dislodging guilt from the clutches of sin, and by necessary consequence, theology, Freud was able to make guilt a biological condition and category to be manipulated. If guilt can be divorced from covenant, there is then no sanctions for man to incur. Man's responsibility to God is loosened and explained away.

As a result of this jockeying about guilt becomes an impulse of the *id* (what we call the sinful "flesh") to be managed by the *ego* (the mind) and *super-ego* (the conscience). Christian theology deals with the sinful flesh of man by making him new in Christ—a reversal of the adamic curse of sin—with the intention on restoring the whole of man, a process of covenantal restoration and holiness. Freud, who rejected religious presuppositions, called it the *id*, *ego*, and *super-ego*, and this was simply man trying to manage his impulses and urges. Embracing the biological and anthropological nature of guilt, Freud presupposed that guilt was nothing but a chemical reaction to be tamed.

However, because man is made in the image of God, he is liable to God: man is unequivocally *responsible* and *accountable*. And yet man in his sin does not want to be subordinate to God so he absolutizes his mission: give-away guilt and all its entanglements *no matter the cost*. The sexual revolution of our day? The culture of death? The insistence on bodily autonomy? All of it is man's attempt at ridding himself of guilt and his accountability to God. Guilt cannot be relegated solely to the mind or solely to biology. It cannot be reduced to mere social constructs and stigmas. *Guilt is theology applied to the whole of man.*

This means that guilt doesn't care about your feelings. It doesn't care about your standard of truth. Guilt comes from God via the law of God and it is entirely unconcerned with regard to what you might think or feel in your attempts to give it away. It is not biological, it is covenantal. If the problem is merely external, then someone else is to blame. If it is merely internal, then we must escape and follow the Greeks. But the truth is it's *both*. A man who is shot feels the pain, no doubt. But before he *feels* the pain, it's an *objective* reality: he's been shot by *someone.* Guilty feelings are downstream from your guilt before God, but it is a guilt-stricken river, nonetheless.

If it's possible for the mind to be tainted by sin to such a degree as to fall into fallacious reasoning, would it not follow that our emotions, similarly tainted by sin, can fall into fallacious feeling? Of course.

One of surest ways we try to manage and rid ourselves of guilt is by giving it away to *false* guilt. Misplaced guilt might just be the most debilitating problem Christians can face. We feel guilty about the things we should not, things that are *lawful*, and then we don't feel guilty about the things that we should, things *unlawful*. This is because of two ditches: on the one side we have licentiousness, and on the other side we have Pharisaism. The reason we fall into these ditches is because we're not sure where to find the road, and this is a result of our spiritual windows being foggy.

When we give away our guilt to false guilt, we are motivated by these two deadly ditches. Sometimes we want to be free in areas we are not permitted to be free. Other times we want to be held captive in ways we are not permitted to be held captive. The underlying commonality of these two ditches on the road to misplaced guilt is the problem of objectivity: we simply don't want to come to grips with the law of God. True guilt pushes us to the gospel for forgiveness and then to the law as a corrective measure. False guilt stumbles in the darkness trying to manage impulses on one's own.

Perhaps you are guilt-driven in your decision-making and relationships because you want to make everyone happy. This false guilt leads you to saying "yes" to everything and "no" to nothing. You want people to like you, to think well of you, so you're willing to compromise what you really think in order to win someone over. You are what the Bible calls, a "double-minded man" (James 1:8; cf. Proverbs 23:7; 26:20). This person is unstable because she has left the law of God in favor of her own foolish, ever-changing standard. With one person she says *this*, with another she says something else. Her guilt is being shifted around instead of dealt with in terms of her relationship to God.

Or perhaps you're in an emotionally unstable place right now so you shut down and try to *think* your way out of feeling guilty. You might be genuinely suffering from depression for dozens of different reasons. But instead of aligning yourself with the law of God you actively retreat in order to stuff the pain. You, too, may just be trying to give your guilt away.

Both persons are giving away their guilt and both are doing so in different ways. Instead of dealing with ourselves and others in terms of God's law we like to create our own standard and expectations, and then force it on others. Let me explain.

False guilt is a temptation because the natural man does not want to come to terms with the reality of being accountable to God. It is easier to feel guilty about the wrong things because the wrong things are created out of thin air. A man could feel absolutely crushed about whales being poached in South Africa, and yet completely fine with abortion and same-sex marriage. True guilt presupposes true righteousness and true justice; false guilt presupposes false righteousness and false justice. False guilt is much more preferable because false righteousness and the false standards contained therein are much more manageable on our terms—they do what *we* want them to do. If you want to know which God you are serving trace your guilt back to the standard of righteousness you claim to adhere to. There is *always* a god of the system. Always. But false guilt is what real guilt uses to get you back to God. The burden of false guilt is much easier to deal with because the idol is *way* more lenient than the Most High.

Recall what we covered already from Romans 3:19. The reason that God shuts the mouths of every person, making them guilty before him, is because God intends to save the world. God doesn't save non-sinners: Jesus came for the sick, not the healthy (Mark 2:17). God is interested in removing our guilt, freeing us from shame, and doing it all based on the work of Jesus Christ. God wants his guilty elect to be freed from this burden.

But the only way to get out of the covenantal state of guilt is through covenantal atonement, and this we simply cannot do on our own. We need justification. We need the declaration of "not guilty" and the other wonderful declaration that goes with it: "*Righteous.*" Either we will run to Christ's atonement in order to be released from true guilt, or we will try to give away our guilt in other ways. One leads to life, the other leads to death (see Pr. 28:1, 17).

But we have a tremendous problem: the Lord *does* count transgressions. David said that a man is blessed when God forgives transgressions and covers sin (Psalm 32:1). But how can a man be forgiven when he is guilty? And how can God be both just and the justifier? If God justifies the guilty, wouldn't that make him an unjust judge, letting us off without punishment? If God punishes us, how can our guilt be expunged? He would then no longer be the type of God who can justify. The answer to this vast problem is the cross of Jesus Christ.

We've already demonstrated that our guilt cannot be assuaged by biological alterations. Freudian thinking is useless. We need something else. We need *someone* else.

Sin can only be dealt with through confession, and confession—the foundation of our faith—coupled with Christ's forgiveness, is a covenantal guarantee from God. Here's what I mean.

We only have two options:

1) We can try and wash ourselves clean, but soap doesn't remove guilty stains (Jeremiah 2:22).
2) We can let the blood of Christ wash us clean and save us from our guiltiness.

Option two is the only true way to accomplish this.

When we confess that Jesus is Lord and believe in our hearts that God raised him from the dead, we, as thinking and feeling creatures, are brought to covenantal restoration. In Christ we are made whole; we are declared to be 'righteous,' and declared 'not guilty.' Justification releases us from sin and its deadly consequences of shame and guilt. But the gospel doesn't *loosen* the chains of guilt, it *destroys* them entirely. You are truly and actually free. You don't have the play the guilt give-away game any longer. God is just and the justifier, and you are free (Rom. 3:26; 8:1).

For the unbeliever stuck in guilt, he can only try to move about, dragging his chains and pretending they don't exist. But in Christ you don't have the chains because they have been destroyed. And even when these chains are broken, there is a very real temptation to create other chains—the chains of false guilt.

For the unbeliever, guilt will erode at his being until he repents or perishes. For the Christian, however, guilt is a good thing because guilt means that the law is at work in our lives, and that our faith and trust in the sufficiency of Christ is at work as well. It's when we don't keep the gospel at the forefront of our thinking and feeling that we start finding ways to give our guilt away.

Instead of dealing with Christ we'd rather sulk in our own self-pity, failing to believe Christ loves us. Instead of being consumed with the love of God in

Christ we'd rather murmur about complaining that things just don't go 'our way,' so we'll take our guilt and place it on others, guilt-tripping them to appease ourselves. If we won't deal with Christ and the abolition of guilt and shame in our lives we're going to be tempted to try and manufacture an idol to soothe our conscience.

Rather than doing this, go to Christ. The next time you feel guilty check to see if there's real guilt or false guilt. Either way, go to Christ. Go to the cross where you have died with him. Go to the tomb where you have been buried with him. Go to the throne where you have been raised with him. *Go to him.* Give him your guilt. Give him your temptations. Give him your sins. And remember that he is faithful and just to forgive us of our sins and cleanse us from all unrighteousness (1 John 1:9). Christ bore your guilt and your shame; don't you *dare* try to pick it back up.

3
EMOTIONAL BAGGAGE FEES

*The thought of my affliction and my homelessness is
wormwood and gall! My soul continually thinks of it and is
bowed down within me. But this I call to mind and
therefore I have hope: The steadfast love of the LORD
never ceases, his mercies never come to an end; they are
new every morning; great is your faithfulness. "The LORD
is my portion," says my soul, "therefore I will hope in
him." The LORD is good to those who wait for him, to
the soul that seeks him. It is good that one should wait
quietly for the salvation of the LORD.*
Lamentations 3:19-26

IT WAS G.K. CHESTERTON WHO ONCE
stated that the trend of good is always towards
incarnation. By this he meant that the indescribable
should become describable, that the unutterable
should become utterable. Chesterton was describing

the arts and philosophy, but I want to take this principle a step further: *The trend of history is always towards greater revelation.*

The Incarnation of Christ the Son of God—the Word who took on flesh—is a remarkable feature of Christian theology. There simply is nothing like it in all the world's religions. But what I find fascinating about it is the fact that *this is consistent with God's self-revelation in history.* God is always moving history along towards greater revelation, greater luminosity, greater *glory*. He is taking man along the road called Revelation, with rest stops of illumination and sanctification along the way.

Obviously the Word would become flesh and dwell among us (John 1:14): Greater light leads to greater revelation which leads to greater clarity on the path to greater glory. All of redemption is a movement from wrath to grace. This is why we call it *grace*; it presupposes wrath.

As we've already covered, man was created in the image of God but forsook this glory by pursuing another glory, one he wanted to define. But this glory turned out to be the equivalent of exchanging an elaborate banquet at a King's table for crumbs at the slave's table. Adam and Eve believed themselves to be free to explore the selfish desires of their hearts.

Instead of trusting God with their emotions, desires, will, and thoughts, they trusted the serpent and brought absolute wreckage to the human race. What started with grace soon after became a movement of history from wrath to grace.

At the center of all this is the fact that part of the wreckage of sin is the emotional scarring that takes place in life. We have emotional baggage fees and they are very much expensive. We have depression and anger, lust and sadness, and these things weigh us down, oftentimes eroding at us to such a degree that we simply cannot function.

This baggage can crush us like Jeremiah described in Lamentations 3. We can be afflicted (vs. 1), driven to darkness (vs. 2), and utterly debilitated (vs. 4). We can feel isolated and alone, weighed down as though in chains (vs. 7). Our emotional baggage can make us feel as helpless as the prey of a bear or lion (vs. 10). Sometimes it's as though everyone is mocking us (vs. 14), and we are thus filled with bitterness (vs. 15). Ever felt so terrible that the only way to describe it is in terms of your teeth grinding on gravel? Jeremiah did (vs. 16). The Bible is full of emotional experience and expression and we would do well to acknowledge it.

As Solomon has taught us there is a time for

everything under heaven (Ecclesiastes 3:1-8). There are times when we must grieve and times we must rejoice. There are times we must experience elation and joy, other times we are faced with utter despondency. While it is true that there is a time and place for these emotions this doesn't mean that experiencing emotion is a bad thing in and of itself. Again, as we talked about in chapter one, we are whole persons with whole bodies with a whole gospel to deal with it all. And this means that our emotions are supposed to work in concert with the rest of our faculties in order to bring glory to God.

To reiterate: we are not to elevate the mind over the emotions, the brain over the heart. We are made in the image of God which means we are thinking, feeling, and doing *creatures*. To exalt one of these equally ultimate features over against the other is to repackage Greek philosophy and call it Christian. And it is most emphatically *not* Christian.

Satan's great plan was the redirection of man's worship, affection, and ambition from God-centeredness to self-centeredness. The *Westminster Larger Catechism*, question number one, asks, "What is the chief and highest end of man?" The answer is, "Man's chief and highest end is to glorify God, and fully to enjoy him forever." When the object of our pursuit of glory and enjoyment is something or someone *other* than the God of the Bible, we have found ourselves worshipping and exalting an idol. All of our worship, all of our affections, all of our ambitions and love and desires are to be *God*-focused. Which means your anger should be God-focused. Your depression, your joy, your frustration and happiness, all of it is to be used to the great end of glorifying God and enjoying him forever. That is your highest aim.

The Bible says a lot about this:

- From him and through him and to him are *all things* (Romans 11:36).
- We were bought with a price which means we are to *glorify* God with our bodies (1 Corinthians 6:20).
- Whether we eat or drink or emote—we must do all of it for the *glory* of God (1 Cor. 10:31).
- All the nations God has made will come and bow down before the LORD and *glorify* his name (Psalm 86:9).
- Our pursuit of knowledge and understanding—which begins with the fear of the LORD (Proverbs 1:7)—must

be to the end of walking in God's truth with an undivided heart persistent on revering God's name (Psalm 86:11).

- Our aim in life, in our thinking and feeling and doing, must be the path of life which leads us to the presence of God where there is fullness of joy and pleasures forevermore (Ps. 16:11).

Which is all to say, our glory-giving purpose *includes* our emotions. If God is moving history along into greater glory and greater clarity, we can rest assured that our emotions are part and parcel to this goal. God wants our emotions to glorify him. Don't stuff them, correct them. Don't ignore them, contextualize them. Don't immaturely wallow in them, grow them with practice and patience.

Before we move on, we need a working definition of what we're talking about. In short: *emotion is simply the soul's way of construing or interpreting a situation.* When a person has concerned himself with a particular thing, the body responds to the thing in both somatic and psychosomatic ways. "Somatic" simply refers to the physiology of the body (Gr. *soma*). Psychosomatic usually refers to the mind. In other words, when you experience something you have *feelings* which leads to *emotions*, which leads to *action*. And this involves both the material and non-material (metaphysical) aspects of our body.

Feelings tend to be our *perception* of something, oftentimes in binary fashion: the thing is good or bad, hot or cold, fun or not-so-fun. 'Feelings' are usually our *immediate* sense perceptions of that which is taking place around us (or in us, too). Oftentimes feelings and emotions are used in a synonymous fashion, but they should be distinguished to some degree. Feelings, you might say, are the prerequisite to emotion: they pave the way to a deeper, more pervasive experience of something. It's one thing to *see* something as a bad situation, recognizing that it is truly bad; it's a completely different thing to go through that situation yourself (e.g., seeing a car accident versus being in the accident).

Emotions usually do two things:

1. They arise in order to help us respond;
2. They help us to be prepared and alert.

Given the complexity of the human body, we can be assured that no one really knows where the metaphysical meets the physical. We don't actually know where our particular *emotional experience* meets the physical *trauma and anxiety* we experience in our gut. When you're depressed, you feel it in your soul, and you feel it in your actual body. Again, this is because we are *whole* persons.

Emotions are given by God and they can be a wonderful gift. Listening closely to your friend describe the turmoil she is currently experiencing should help you to be empathic in your response. Remember: emotions prepare us for action, and they help us respond to an experience. Your empathy in responding to someone in need is a wonderful feature to living in God's world, something we should probably cultivate even more than we do.

But emotions are not neutral, and they will either serve the end of God's glory, or they will not, which means that emotions can by sinfully positioned. Your friend might be sharing her feelings on a particularly difficult situation she is experiencing and instead of listening and being a good friend, you might whisper to your mind, and then your other friend later on, "Well she brought this on herself and because she's too stubborn to see it; I can't help her."

Sinners tend to respond sinfully to being sinned

against, after all, sin is *always* crouching at the door. But it is also true that sinners can respond sinfully to *not* being sinned against. Depending on our emotional intelligence and maturity in the moment we may not be able to actually help our friend and be a good listener because we're too busy criticizing and trying to "fix" them. And for the sake of argument, you may be right, she might be extremely stubborn. But gossiping or whispering isn't going to help the situation. Be a good friend not a whisperer (Prov. 16:28; 18:8).

Now, emotions are complex instruments. You can, in a single moment, experience a rush of emotions. The first time I stepped foot on African soil was a flurry of emotion: excitement, nervousness, awe, and uncertainty. It is very much possible to have mixed emotions, and this is because we are persons who come from *the* Person. God is the Absolute Personality who thinks and feels and acts. Jesus himself had mixed emotions! But the way we deal with the complexity is developing the maturity and self-control needed to *understand* them, which means we can then *wield them properly*. We want to use our emotions, not have our emotions use us.

The purpose of emotions is really quite simple.

God has given us emotions in order to *communicate* (especially things that are important to us), to aid in *relating* to one another, to move us towards righteous *action* in the world, and to help us *worship* God. The essence of man isn't emotion, but we have emotion. Again, we're *whole persons*. But we are to use our emotions in Godly ways.

Sometimes we need to express what we value which means emotions can be used to communicate what we 'think' or feel. Other times we need to be able to relate to one another and since we're not heartless robots, we need emotion to deepen our experience of each other. Sometimes we need the right emotion to move us towards the dominion mandate. And lastly, God made us in his image which means the worship and glory he wants from us should be passionate, not rote.

(The Stoics believed in *apatheia*, which is the Greek word that literally means "without passion." Their aim, as we touched on in chapter one, was to reach a state of mind wherein the passions would be tamed and set aside. However, contrary to this erroneous view of emotion, God desires that we desire; he longs for our longing, not because he lacks anything but because he is our greatest good and we should definitely get excited about that prospect.)

The title of this chapter is "Emotional Baggage Fees" and I chose this name because I want to make sure we deal with all the ways we fall short in our experience of emotion. For example, sometimes we find ourselves in a state of:

- *Denial*: "I can't possibly feel upset about this situation, after all, it's not my burden to carry."
- *Minimizing*: "I don't need to feel *that* bad about it."
- *Blaming*: "It was really her fault anyway."
- *Rationalizing/Intellectualizing*: "I shouldn't feel this way, after all, there's a logical reason to why this happened."
- *Distracting*: "I'm not going to let myself feel this way, so I'll keep myself busy doing something else."
- *Over-reacting/being hostile*: "I feel betrayed so I'm going to pay this person back."
- *Projection*: "In my bitterness towards this person, I'm going to believe that she hates me."

All of these reactions lack maturity and that's because they lack self-control.

One of the greatest ways to exhibit self-control is to stop and ask the question, "What does God require of me in this moment?" *How does God want me to think right now? How does he want me to feel? What is/are my current emotion(s) telling me about me? What is/are my current emotion(s) telling me about my view of God? What is/are my current emotion(s) telling me about this person I am called to love and serve?*

If you can ask this and respond accordingly, you will have the ability to see clearly and respond in a godly way. And make no mistake: self-control is at the center of all of this. God wants us to respond to things emotionally, but it has to be the correct emotion, not the wrong one. Which is to say, we're supposed to be emotionally healthy and mature people.

In order to deal with the baggage fees and their desultory wandering about inflicting harm on ourselves and others, we have to remember that we must grow up. We have to love God with our mind, body, heart, soul, strength, and *emotions* (cf. Deuteronomy 6:4-7, Matthew 22:37-40, Mark 12:30-31, and Luke 10:27). God wants us to be mature exhibiting emotionally healthy patterns that reflect the Lord Jesus Christ. Sometimes that emotion is anger, other times it is pure joy. Either way, the emotion is to be healthy, ethically pure, and in line with the Scriptures.

Being mature and emotionally healthy looks like the following: Articulating your thoughts and feelings honestly, clearly, directly, and humbly. It looks like you taking responsibility for your thoughts, emotions, and actions. It means that under stress and consternation you are able to say what you mean, and mean what you say, without being an adversarial jerk.

Being a Spirit-filled, emotionally healthy person means considering others and what they are saying and *not* saying before you react and respond. This requires you having an empathetic disposition without jumping to conclusions, respecting them enough to hear them out without trying to manage them. Emotional health is also tied to physical health: are you eating right? Are you getting proper exercise, etc.? Are you taking control of your physical body or giving yourself over to sloth?

Emotionally healthy people are people who are in tune with all of these things to the degree that they live comfortably in the will of God, secure in their identity in Christ, walking day by day, patiently waiting on the Lord (Ps. 46:10).

Despite the impressive suffering Jeremiah had to endure, he had the sense and maturity to keep all of those emotions in check for the end of the glory of God. He called to mind and therefore had hope: "The steadfast love of the LORD never ceases, his mercies never come to an end; they are new every morning; great is your faithfulness. 'The LORD is my portion,' says my soul, 'therefore I will hope in him.' The LORD is good to those who wait for him, to the soul that seeks him. It is good that one should wait quietly for the salvation of the LORD."

In all of our emotional despondency—the highs and the lows—we can trust the Lordship of Jesus Christ in and over our emotions. The New Heavens and New Earth isn't going to be a place where our emotions are eradicated; it's going to be an experience where our emotions are completely and freely, perfectly—you might say—*expressed*. The cross of Christ is sufficient to restore us to himself, and the "us" most assuredly includes our obstinate emotions.

4
ENVIRONMENTALISM

They heard the sound of the Lord God walking in the garden at the time of the evening breeze, and the man and his wife hid themselves from the presence of the Lord God among the trees of the garden. But the Lord God called to the man, and said to him, "Where are you?" He said, "I heard the sound of you in the garden, and I was afraid, because I was naked; and I hid myself." He said, "Who told you that you were naked? Have you eaten from the tree of which I commanded you not to eat?" The man said, "The woman whom you gave to be with me, she gave me fruit from the tree, and I ate." Then the Lord God said to the woman, "What is this that you have done?" The woman said, "The serpent tricked me, and I ate."
Genesis 3:8–13

AS WE SAW IN CHAPTER TWO, GUILT AND responsibility belong together because *guilt is incurred when responsibility is forsaken.* When Adam and Eve chose to forgo their responsibility to work and keep the garden in obedience to God, they incurred guilt for having transgressed the law of God. This autonomous impulse is at the center of all pagan thinking and philosophizing. With God and his covenant thrown aside, man's ascendancy will inexorably follow. In fact, history's great antithesis is the interminable jostling of thrones and dominion: *Who's in charge? To whom do I report?* Is man in charge, and thus sovereign, or is God the sovereign in this relationship? The futility of man's attempts to de-throne God is shown in the revival of paganism, especially paganism's attempt at assuaging man's guilty conscience.

One of the foremost ways sinful man tries to relieve his guilt is by blaming his environment. Take the incident at the forbidden tree in Eden. When God asked about Adam's nakedness and if he had eaten from the forbidden tree, Adam replied, "The *woman* whom *you* gave to be with me, she gave me from the tree, and I ate." The guile in Adam's heart is now on display for all to see. In his guilt Adam attempted to appease his conscience by blaming God's apparently deficient gifts. Eve, who was given to Adam as a preeminent gift, was now to blame for Adam's bad decision. Not to be outdone, Eve, when asked the same thing, decided to blame the serpent who had deceived her. Both parties claimed that their environment was the cause of their transgression, and thus both parties ignored their individual, moral culpability for their sin.

Paganism itself believes in what we can call a "closed universe." That man exists inside an impersonal, indifferent universe is the predominant feature of pagan thought. If there is no sovereign personality governing man, then there must be no such thing as a personal universe either. An impersonal universe means there is no meaning and therefore, no accountability. Without meaning man is free to blame his environment, after all, "Evolution made me like this." Without accountability man is free to determine his own purpose because, after all, naturalistic evolution is purposeless. This closed universe thinking means that the earth is all we have, and death just *is*. Chance governs us all and fate is her handmaiden.

Pagan belief in such nonsense requires a whole lot of environmental philosophy. If we are simply bags of protoplasm and neurons firing about, products of time and chance acting on cells and matter, then whatever happens is the result of a relativized chain-of-being in which everything is to be self-determined instead of God-determined. In this world predestination and imputation are nothing but self-contrived processes. It's not that we're simply spontaneous creatures, we're spontaneous creatures who have the obligation (*who says?*) to create our own world. This existential drive forces man to adopt his own sovereignty and explain away his existence all apart from the Creator God.

But the Bible speaks of no such thing. The God of the Bible asserts his superiority in and through history. He is the Creator of the *world*. Every atom and molecule moves about governed by the Sovereignty of Jehovah. This is not a universe governed by chance; it's a universe governed by a *personal* God. His sovereignty over and through time results in what theologians call "first and second causes." God has given us the freedom to choose that which he has predestined. We are free as *secondary*, wholly derived creatures to move about in history with purpose and meaning, but this moving about can only be such to the degree that it acknowledges and worships the Lordship of Jesus Christ.

Even so, this also means that the Tri-personal Godhead has a law attached to his person. In order to be sovereign, he must have a law-word and we find this in the Bible. This fact alone completely eradicates any possible success-mission of man's usurpation of God. Man will *try* to rid himself of

God and revolt against the maturity God requires of him, however, this will be entirely unsuccessful because man is a finite *creature*. Newsflash: we're second fiddle.

Man's creatureliness means that man is accountable and responsible to God and his law. *He cannot blame his environment for his plight.* As James 4:1 asks, "Those conflicts and disputes among you, where do they come from? Do they not come from your cravings [passions] that are at war within you?" It is not what goes into a man that pollutes him, it's what comes out: it's what comes from the heart—the center of a man—that taints and blemishes him. *We are not primarily products of our environment;* we are created to create, produced to produce, caused in order to cause. We are *personal* beings who come from the *Personal Being.*

Now, let's get a little practical on how environmentalism tends to work itself out. You may have grown up in a terrible home: abusive parents, promiscuous parents, or addicted parents. Verbal, emotional, and physical abuse may have marked your childhood. Husbands who run out on their wives, wives who run out on their husbands—these are the environments in which many people have been raised. Perhaps your parents never taught you how to handle conflict or how to manage money. Perhaps you were bullied in public school. It is quite possible that some form of sexual abuse came about in your childhood. Nevertheless, these grievous sins should *not* be seen as things that *determine* who you are.

In the first chapter of this book I traced the difference between the pagan construction of the world and Christian theology. The pagan sees man as a product of chaos and his environment. Christian doctrine teaches that man is a product of the living God, made in his image. Our being and nature is *God*-determined not *self*-determined. This distinction is absolutely necessary for dealing with emotions, addictions, and trials. We are not made in the image of our environment.

It goes without saying that we must deal with family of origin issues. You have to deal with the fact that you've been betrayed by someone, hurt by someone, perhaps crushed by someone. Somewhere along the line you have been affected by someone else's sins. Families can be tremendous blessings and horrific curses, depending on the holiness of its members. That said, we must not discredit or downplay those "environmental" circumstances. Instead of pushing them aside, ignoring them or pretending they don't exist, we need to be able to filter them through a proper theology. To reiterate what I said in chapter one:

> We must deal with the trauma: the hurt, the betrayal, the rejection, the feelings of being unloved or unwanted, and the pain. Like it or not, those things shape us and mold us—they are influencers, not determiners. They impact us, but they don't define us. We are made in the image of God, planted here to grow and mature and reflect God's thinking, God's feeling, and God's purposes. Don't reject the world, see it as broken and in need of restoration. The same can be said of you.

Let's get even more practical for a moment. Instead of blame shifting everything to our environment we're going to instead embrace the environment, knowing that all along, God was and is in control. These things shape us, no doubt, and we would be wise to see them. Here's a non-comprehensive list of possible environmental factors that have shaped your emotional maturity, or lack thereof:

- *Family* — Your parents did a lot for you so you owe them everything, thus making an idol out of what should be considered a good gift from God. Or, maybe the family "name" was such an unrelenting source of focus that you constantly sought to please your parents no matter the cost, regardless of what you thought to be true or felt to be right. You could never really please them, so you're crushed under the weight of performance. Your family took priority over the Kingdom. Or perhaps the flip side is true: you grew up in a very disjointed family with abuse and quarreling, a fractured "family" who could never quite get things right. To this day it bothers you.

- *Relationships* — You don't trust people. Ever. This is because people have let you down so many times you have guarded yourself. You can't fathom any more emotional hurt, so you never let anyone in. The opposite could be true: you long for friendship so you're willing to say anything to anyone, but no one really knows the real you.

- *Success* — The rat race of having the biggest, best, and most expensive stuff drives you. You call it postmillennial progress but it's really greed. You want to make a lot of money because you have something to prove to your parents, your friends, or your false god. Instead of Kingdom faithfulness, you're after your own kingdom. This, too, could have an opposite dysfunction: you're lazy and slothful, never able to get things done because you've never learned your individual purpose in the Kingdom of God.

- *Sex* — Perhaps your parents never taught you a thing and you've always grown up thinking sexuality was a terrible topic never to be discussed. This confusion may have led you to explore sexuality in sinful ways and this has wreaked havoc on your self-esteem. Due to your past, sexual frustration sets in and as a result, you are unable to grow close to your spouse. Your false expectations have led to false views about men and women and lust consumes you.

- *Conflict* — You grew up in a passive home, which meant that conflict was to be avoided at all cost. You people-please in order to get people to like you and escape their wrath. Or maybe you grew up in a loud home where everyone shouted all the time and conflict resolution looked more like a knock-down, drag-out fight. Either way, you have no clue how to be a peacemaker or how to own your sin and help overlook the sin in others. Matthew 18 means nothing to you.

- *Anger* — The emotionally precarious person flips out at the sign of any perceived instability. You love control and the minute you sense a lack of it you lose your mind and the volcano erupts. You don't know how to speak softly because no one ever spoke to you that way. Sometimes you give yourself over to sarcasm and tittle-tattle because you're afraid of your anger because of what you've done with it.

There are dozens and dozens of things we could

look at, and this list merely scratches the surface. The point, however, is quite clear. Family of origin issues *do* affect us in ways we are oftentimes unable to perceive. The way our parents acted and reacted gives us an unconscious look into how things *should* or *shouldn't* be. For example, your parents were passive and never talked about problems, so you just assume that's the only way to go about things. You get the picture.

The reason we need have a healthy view of our environment, whether its family of origin, your current life stage, your relationships, etc., is because our emotions are uniquely connected to these experiences and these experiences tend to shape us in ways we usually don't anticipate. The child whose insecurity drives him to seek approval from his habitually absent father will impact him as he grows. Like it or not we all have emotional baggage and we all are influenced to a great degree by our environment.

But it's one thing to identify the issues, it's another thing to deal with them. How should we go about handling ourselves in light of newfound revelation?

The first thing I would suggest is to remember the theological underpinnings of what we've just considered: environment is sovereignly orchestrated by God—the good and the bad—and God desires our maturation through the struggles. The bad stuff should be seen as bad stuff and growth means knowing the difference. These problems aren't problems that are untouchable, they are problems God can and will solve. When David sinned, he didn't blame others; his repentance was deep and that's because it was ultimately against *God* (Psalm 51:4). The same can be said for the sins of others that affect us. Those sins are sins against *God* first, then others. If you have bitterness in your heart towards your family or towards your spouse, the only way out is repentance and forgiveness and that's going to require a lot of work.

Another thing I would suggest is taking the time to sit down with a good friend who is willing to listen and help sift through the emotional struggles you're experiencing. You don't really know someone until you've asked them this question: "What is your experience of me?" This type of humility and transparency is very difficult because it requires us to open ourselves for examination. *And no one likes to be this vulnerable.*

The way out of the emotional trap of your environment is by dealing with God *first*, confessing any unrepentant sin, and *second*, sifting through the struggle with a friend who's willing to potentially wound you. Remember: that's faithfulness according to Scripture (Prov. 27:6). Working through the environment instead of blaming the environment is the key to a healthy heart.

In all that we feel—all the consternation and joy, hurt and happiness—we must give ourselves over to biblical thinking and biblical feeling. No environment is so bad that God cannot overcome. No upbringing is so bad that you can't labor in Christ to go a different route. No hurt is so deep that your Savior can't empathize with. No emotional scarring is so bad that the balm of our union with Christ cannot heal.

You are not a product of your environment: you are a human being made in the image of God, and Christ has come to see to it that this image is fully restored.

5
PRESSING DEPRESSION

*As a deer longs for flowing streams, so my soul longs for
you, O God. My soul thirsts for God, for the living God.
When shall I come and behold the face of God? My tears
have been my food day and night,
while people say to me continually, "Where is your God?"
These things I remember, as I pour out my soul: how I
went with the throng, and led them in procession to the
house of God, with glad shouts and songs of thanksgiving, a
multitude keeping festival. Why are you cast down, O my
soul, and why are you disquieted within me? Hope in God;
for I shall again praise him, my help and my God.*
Psalm 42:1-6a

HAVING DEALT WITH THE WORLDVIEW
foundations in chapter one, the great problem of
guilt in chapter two, the reality of emotional baggage
in chapter three, and the problems that face us if we
take an environmental approach to dealing with our
emotions in the last chapter, we now come to the
final chapter dealing with perhaps the most pressing

emotional issue of our day: *depression*.

I have called this chapter "pressing depression" not only because it is a *pressing* matter—it's debilitating consequences can be truly dreadful—but because depression ought to *pressed*, that is, analyzed and examined and investigated. Like any emotional condition there are a variety of factors that can contribute to this particular affliction. I am convinced that depression is wildly misunderstood and because of that, Christians are largely unequipped to help those who suffer from it.

Depression is a difficult topic to address and must be done so with humility and caution. There is no way I can say to you that this is the final word on the matter. However, the Christian Church doesn't really deal much with it, so I felt it necessary to offer my feeble attempt. Having suffered from anxiety several years ago and having various bouts with despondency and uncertainty over the years, I can say that I have tasted a *smidgen* of depression; I have personally never had the main course, but I have had the hors d'oeuvres.

The first thing we need to realize is that the Bible *does* say a lot about depression. Several biblical characters suffered from various symptoms of depression: Moses (Numbers 11:14) and Jeremiah

(Lamentations 3); Elijah (1 Kings 19:1-18); Job (e.g., Job 6:2-3), and many of the psalmists (42:1-11; 77; 88). But one thing needs to be clear: there is no *one* cause, nor is there only *one* solution. It's far more complex than that.

We've already emphasized several times over that we are *whole* persons. This means that the mental, physical, and emotional parts of our being are intertwined and not always easily identified. Who but God knows the exact place where the immaterial meets the material, or where the brain's neurons meet your emotional depression? To ask the question is to answer it. There are three main aspects of the body when it comes to identifying the causes of depression: Mind, body, soul.

Regarding the *mind*, depression can be a combination of chemical imbalance and wrong thinking. One could suffer from depression because of a brain that lacks physical health, perhaps cerebral spinal fluid is blocked, or your dopamine levels are off. He could also suffer because he has given himself over to fear or bitterness. Depression, it needs to be stressed, is *not* always a result of some secret sin(s). The mind is rather complex which means we ought not to be flippantly dismissive in our conclusions.

Regarding the *body*, it is safe to say that eating

McDonald's every single day isn't going to contribute to a healthy lifestyle. Vitamin deficiencies can wreak havoc on your mental, emotional, and physical state. One article I recently read cited a study that showed the connection between eating healthy and mood change. Gut health contributes to healthy skin, healthy bones, and every other organ, why would we think the brain would be any different?

While it is legitimate (in theory) that chemical imbalances in the brain can be treated with chemicals correctives, it is also clear that Big-Pharma is a Statist's utopia for pushing pills instead of promoting a holistic approach to dealing with your body. Getting proper nutrition helps your *physical* body; no doubt it can help your *emotional* and *mental* 'body' as well. One example will suffice.

A study I found shows that your gut is responsible for generating 95% of your serotonin and 50% of your dopamine; it also contributes to building healthy levels of melatonin and adrenaline.[*] You literally have 4-5 pounds of bacteria in your gut, and *all* of it is connected to the rest of your body. Do not underestimate the power of food!

_____

[*] https://www.ncbi.nlm.nih.gov/pmc/articles/PMC4662178/ (Accessed August 19, 2019).

Regarding the *soul*, it is clear from Scripture that depression can be caused by a variety of things: demonic influence and possession, sin, persecution, emotional abuse, etc.

The trouble comes in when we take any of these aspects of the body and suggest that one is cured or caused by the other. In other words, wrong *assumptions* lead to wrong *solutions*. Emotional well-being is just as important as mental well-being. For far too long Christians have been working with faulty assumptions about the human body, and as a result, they have come up with horrendous solutions to the emotional weight each of us carries.

For example, we here at Cross & Crown Church in Northern Virginia believe in Nouthetic counseling. The word "nouthetic" comes from the Greek word we normally translate in English as "admonish," or "correct." Nouthetic counseling is helpful in terms of pushing us to think biblically. However, it can be unhelpful if we assume that depression is solely the result of hidden, unconfessed sin. Again: that *could* be the case. Someone might have a secret addiction that is causing all sorts of problems in her life. But we have to be careful not to assume that just because someone is feeling down in the dumps that he or she is sinning behind closed doors.

As we have seen, depression can sometimes be a seemingly impenetrable thing. The writer of our passage here in Psalm 42 tries to deal with feelings of despondency. He knows that God is his only hope, so he longs like a deer searching for water (v. 1). Because of his parched state of despondency, his soul thirsts for God (v. 2). Probably unable to eat, he cries night and day and thus his tears are his food (v. 3). There is outside persecution that has crippled him, people mocking him asking where his God is to be found (v. 3). Despite his depressive state, he presses in and remembers some things while pouring out his soul (v. 4). He then speaks to himself, instead of listening to himself, and asks his soul, "Why are you cast down?" (v. 5). He recalls to mind his purpose and goal: to hope in God, for God is his help. Which means that *emotional lamentation is a gift that God is quite capable of handling*, so feel free to lament yourself to sleep—it's part of the process.

Pressing depression requires us to take seriously every aspect of our being. Because of sin, our soul aches for the image of God to be made right, whole, and complete. While it is true that we live in a fallen world where mental breakdowns occur, where sugar addictions are rampant, where dopamine and serotonin levels run amuck, where right thinking and feeling and doing oftentimes runs contrary to the will of God—*we must recall to mind the restorative nature of the gospel of the Kingdom.* Does the Bible have answers to every area of life or not? If so, are we dealing with God in our suffering and frustration? Or idealizing and dreaming and refusing obedience in the midst of the struggle?

What God is doing in the world through the gospel of Jesus Christ is bringing healing and restoration to the brokenness: *far as the curse is found.* There is a careful balance that needs to be made here. We need not *underestimate* the grip depression has on people by saying things like, "Well, God is good, you just need to pray more." Or, "Get over it, stop being selfish." You *might* need to remember the goodness of God in prayer. You *might* be selfish, and this is a sin. But we must also never *overestimate* the grip depression has on people by saying things like, "You'll never recover, just keep popping pills." Or, "There's absolutely nothing you can do, so keep binge-eating all hours of the night." Once more, we need balance.

Part of the process of balancing means avoiding the extremes, avoiding the tendency to over-generalize. Committing one sin doesn't mean you've left the faith nor does making one mistake at work mean you're an utter failure. Sometimes we're prone to focusing on the negative more than the positive. Other times we take the positive and bend it into a negative. Sometimes we develop an unhealthy fixation on others, constantly pointing out their faults in hopes that it will make us feel better about ourselves. Or perhaps we are insecure and thus we withdraw from others.

We can also give ourselves over to hasty assumptions about other people especially towards those with whom we do life on the regular. We have an experience with someone, say, a friend who was late to your meeting, and you assume she doesn't like you anymore. Or perhaps he didn't text you back because he was busy at work, but you assume his intentions, rehearsing them over and over again in your head.

Sometimes our feelings of hopelessness and despair are so strong that we adopt pagan thinking, hoping it will help. We might adopt the mindset that we can *predict* how things are going to be based on our feelings. We toss out the mental in favor of the emotional—as if one is more important than the other. This could be someone thinking that depression is sin, and since they're a sinner, they'll never get out of sin. This cycle of despair can be driven by an incessant need to be liked and loved, and when someone doesn't get what they think they deserve, they pity themselves and never press the depression; they instead *embrace* the depression.

Other times we're given over to the performance-driven life. We're the firstborns with perfectionism problems. We have unhealthy expectations of ourselves which leaves us crippled in despair because we can never quite get it right. Our aim is to out-perform the next person and then criticize them for failing to be "like us."

Lastly, there is tendency in Christian thinking to take on responsibility when we simply are not called to do so. For example, our kid acts out and we rush to the extreme of thinking we're a complete failure of a parent. Or, our lack of repentance has us failing to believe the truth of, say, 1 John 1:9, which says that God is faithful to forgive us when we confess to him.

All of these things *can* contribute to depression; *none of them can solve it.* All of them can contribute to the messy garage, and suddenly you walk into it one day wondering how it got so bad. We need right *thinking* and part of the right thinking is fighting for *biblical thinking* in the process. This can be incredibly challenging, especially for severe cases of depression.

Having said all that, it is important to treat depression in a holistic manner. There can be an abundance of causes: sin, stress, false expectations, lifestyle, life events, traumatic events, unhealthy patterns of sleep, terrible eating habits, crisis of faith, false self-images, unbiblical psychology, constant sickness, and wrong-headed thinking about life and relationships.

Given the fact that the *causes* can be vast, we can safely conclude that the *treatment* is just as broad. One person can be depressed because of terrible decisions he or she made at work, thus reaping the consequences. Another person can be depressed because of a traumatic event in his family. Either way, the treatments are going to be wide and varied, and we should see to it that we press the depression, that is, explore it so we can do our best to treat it.

It's important to keep these things in front of us so as to help those who are feeling down. But let me offer a clarification: I am convinced that some level of depression or anxiety is normal for Christians. The reason I say this is because we are redeemed souls living in the middle of a grand renovation project. Christ is putting all enemies under his footstool; he's putting an end to things like depression and cancer, sickness and anxiety. However, the end is *not yet*. This renovation of the cosmos is currently underway, which means we still have to deal with the difficulties—the traffic jams, the detours, the road closures and orange cones. We have to deal with the trials and tribulations. We have to deal with the depression. We have to juggle and balance life in a world where redemption is underway.

Which means we need to establish healthy patterns in every area of life. We need *emotional* health, cultivating things like encouragement towards others, joy, peace, self-sacrifice, service, and love. We need *physical* health, cultivating things like nutrition, exercise, and holistic foods. We need *spiritual* health, cultivating things like Bible reading and prayer, Sabbath and worship.

For example, if your prayer life is virtually non-existent, you're going to have much difficulty. We must be on guard keeping watch over our souls and one of the ways we do this is by praying without ceasing (1 Thess. 5:17). Our lives ought to be marked by constant Bible study, constant prayer, and things like scripture memorization (Ps. 119:9). If we're going to guard our minds, we must do so with the helmet of salvation (Eph. 6:17). Silence and solitude before the Lord are a must. Cultivating patterns of economic development for the currency of the soul is crucial to living in this bankrupt world.

But what about the physical? Has God given us a pattern for living? Yes, he has, and it's called *Sabbath.* Living simply, taking a break, going on vacation, eating proper foods, spending time outside—all of these things can be healthy patterns of Sabbath. Rest itself is a pattern God has placed in creation in order to bless us and keep us. We would do well to rest well. And we would also do well to acknowledge that God has given us each a dominion purpose, yet, this calling isn't to be a burden, but a blessing. The pursuit of our individual calling is a must, but the *way* we pursue it should be healthy, too.

Developing healthy patterns is a fight. It's a fight to do the things we may not want to do. It can be challenging to put our phones down and enjoy the family. It can be difficult to get out of bed when you've stayed up far too late when you know you have to work in the morning. It can be a real bear sometimes, grabbing your bible and opening it up, instead of reading the latest drama on Facebook. And the reason is oftentimes because of unhealthy patterns being easier than healthy ones.

The messy garage of your emotional state didn't just magically appear one day. Day after day, week after week, you've placed things there not realizing at the time that the accumulation of emotional junk has built up. Changing these patterns means taking out the trash: stop hoarding things like jealousy and bitterness. Stop holding on to self-pity and anger. Fight to keep the garage clean by repenting of self-righteousness, unbelief, and carelessness.

But we can also help others keep their garage cleaned up by recalling to mind Romans 13:8, which says, "Owe no one anything, except to love one another; for the one who loves another has fulfilled the law."

There is an economic paradigm to our relationship with others and with ourselves. There are deposits and credits, withdrawals and profit margins. The good habits can be tremendous credits in your life—rest, worship, prayer, encouragement towards others, etc. The bad habits can be horrific withdrawals—bitterness, anger, neglect of spiritual care, etc. But the only thing we owe to one another is love, that is, the lawful treatment of one another. But it isn't a cold, lawful treatment of one another; it's a passionate, self-giving treatment of one another. It's the garage cleaning. It's the refusal to let unhealthy stuff accumulate by overlooking offenses, a love which covers a multitude of sins. It's a refusal to let your garage's mess spill into the garages of others. Store the good stuff in your life not the messy stuff. And this will require you, like the psalmist, to fight for joy, for peace, for happiness and contentment.

One final thing. If there's one thing we've learned thus far, it's that the answer to emotional despondency isn't stuffing our emotions. It's not that we're *too* emotional; it's that we're not emotional *enough*. In our empathy and witness towards the world and each other; towards victims of abuse and the like—were not emotional enough! We should be far angrier about injustice and abuse. We should be far more emotionally charged about the Kingdom of God's advancement on the earth.

Instead of suppressing our emotions, fight for the right ones, especially in moments of despondency. Fight for the centrality of the gospel in your life. Fight for the centrality of the gospel of the *Kingdom* in your life. Labor with purpose and vision, passion and vitality. Cultivate passion and meaning. Keep your focus on the one who died to forgive you and *restore* you.

EPILOGUE

*It is good for me that I was **humbled**,*
so that I might learn your statutes.
Psalm 119:71

SOME TRANSLATIONS SAYS THAT IT WAS good [David] was "afflicted" so he can learn God's statutes. The NRSV says "humbled," yet the ESV and NASB both say "afflicted." Why?

The Hebrew verb is *'anah* and it carries the idea of someone being brought low in affliction and suffering. Both translations work depending on the context. David is clearly "humbled," as in, "brought low." He is afflicted, bowed down, oppressed, and brought low. But why?

It is always helpful to read the Bible in context and this passage is no different. In verse 66 David asks God to "teach me good judgment and knowledge," for "I believe in your commandments." He says in very next verse, "Before I was humbled [same word] I went astray, but now I keep your word." It is quite possible that David is reflecting on his great sin against God, Bathsheba, and Uriah—a defining moment in his life. He goes on to speak of the "arrogant" who "smear me with lies" (vs. 69); "their hearts are fat and gross," but David "delight[s] in [God's] law" (vs. 70).

Regardless of *what* David is reflecting on, it is clear from the context that he is experiencing great affliction from his walking astray (vs. 67). His departure from God and his law-word has led him to be brought low and humbled. Despite this emotional despondency, David can call it "good" because it has led him closer to God. Even in his sin, God uses the guilt and feelings of remorse to bring us closer to him. The *reason* David saw his affliction as "good" is for the end of "learn[ing] [God's] statues" (vs. 71).

David's estrangement from the Lord because of his sin is considered a good thing because through it, he learned God's statutes. Had David *not* gone through this very emotional experience, he wouldn't have learned—at least not in the same way.

The point I want to make here at the end of this

book has everything to do with the sovereignty of God in your life. Your emotions—and I mean *all your emotions*—are tools God uses to teach us. He has made us to be creatures who express emotion. And we've already seen all the ways we fail to emote the right way! Even still, God desires to work in and through your emotions, and he demonstrates this in the life of David, the poor wretched sinner who was brought low and then exalted. David's life was meticulously predestined in such a way as to bring glory to God in and through the depression, despondency, and anxiety. The affliction was for *good*. The only way you can say this if Christ is on the throne. You cannot say that affliction is 'good' if evolution is true. You cannot say that affliction is 'good' if the universe is a random accident. You cannot say that affliction is 'good' if the Greek philosophers are correct in their view of man.

But you can call everything 'good' if the Creator God is working in and through history, in and through the suffering, in order to bring you to greater intimacy and knowledge of his son, the Lord Jesus Christ.

If God is for us, who can be against us?

So, dear reader, by all means, be emotional. But be emotional in all the *right* ways.

To ensure that man's rebellious tendencies are brought to frustration each and every time, God has built within the framework of his work in history a remarkable principle that will always accomplish the goal of humbling man: "What do you have that you did not receive?" (1 Corinthians 4:7).

The answer, of course, is *nothing*.

ABOUT THE AUTHOR

Dr. Jason Garwood has spent his career seeking to both understand and apply the Biblical worldview to every single area of life. His aim is to help pastors and churches to be better equipped to engage in the Great Commission by teaching Christians how to find their individual purpose in the Kingdom of God and learn how to identify and respond to cultural idols.

He is currently the teaching pastor at Cross & Crown Church in Northern Virginia:

- Cross & Crown was planted in 2017 with a vision and mission to equip men, women, and children to press the crown rights of King Jesus into every area of life;
- Cross & Crown is a house-church movement seeking to establish other house churches across the world; and
- Cross & Crown is laboring to promote liberty and justice by local activism and involvement in the community.

He is a writer and activist:

- Jason is the author of four books, including *Reconstructing the Heart* and *The Politics of Humanism*;
- He has written articles for various outlets and blogs at jasongarwood.com; and
- He has preached and lectured internationally on a variety of subjects, exposing the underling errors and problems with anti-biblical worldviews such as: government education, the drug war, the police state, humanist philosophy, and vaccines;
- You can find him at college campuses, high schools, and political meetings seeding the gospel of the Kingdom of Jesus Christ.

Most importantly, Jason is a devoted husband and father:

- He has been married to his wife, Mary, for 13 years;
- They have three children;
- He makes his home in Warrenton, Virginia.

NOTES:

NOTES:

NOTES:

NOTES:

NOTES:

NOTES:

NOTES:

Made in the USA
Coppell, TX
10 March 2021